Introduction by W. Terrence Gordon

Ten years after explaining television in *Understanding Media*, McLuhan moves, in this piece, to a speculation reserved there for the computer: "the advent of TV may carry us beyond speech altogether." This is neither idle speculation nor showy prophecy, and McLuhan quotes Caleb Gattegno's *Towards a Visual Culture* to buttress his claim, turning it into the inevitable conclusion for media effects deriving from the power of human sight and constraints on the structure of human language: "In contrast to the speed of light, we need time to talk and to express what we want to say." Gattegno's observation relates to what the Swiss linguistic pioneer Ferdinand de Saussure referred to as "the linearity of the signifier," a notion akin to the "one-at-a-timeness" that McLuhan contrasted with "all-at-onceness" in speaking of the transition from mechanical to electric hegemony in the galaxy of media effects. In the same year that he would discover on his own the relevance of Saussure's thought on language to his own thoughts on all media, McLuhan detected in Gattegno's words an argument to support the projection that the long-range and enduring effects of television could move human communication beyond conventional verbal language. In the closing paragraphs of this essay, inspired by one of the biggest news stories of the twentieth century, McLuhan invites us to stop thinking about Sputnik and start thinking about what constitutes "news," bringing us thus to see that there are no media without media interaction. Among rich reflexions on this theme come still more on the relation of cognition to recognition, the alteration and extension of perceptions, and the technological imperative of Lapp's Law: "If it can be done, it's got to be done." Sputnik does not vanish from sight amid McLuhan's intellectual comets, and he tells us that what is inseparable from the closing of the gap between experience and meaning is spectator participation. Sputnik and the new environment it created also created a new content for that environment.--WTG

At the Moment of Sputnik the Planet became a Global Theater in which there are no Spectators but only Actors

In 1901 a message was read to a group at the gate of Windsor Castle:

'Her Majesty the Queen breathed her last at 6:30 p.m., surrounded by her children and grandchildren.'

Pandemonium broke loose. A yelling stampede of journalists on bicycles hurtled down the hill to Cowes to be first with the telephones, bawling as they went, "Queen dead!" "Queen dead!" The famous 'hush'which had always surrounded 'The Widow of Windsor' was shattered at a blow. A new age had begun. [3]

---

1 Longford, Elizabeth. *Victoria R. I.* London: Weidenfeld & Nicholson, 1964, p. 562.

Declining to write for the *Revue Européenne* in 1831, Lamartine said to its editor:

> Do not perceive in these words a superb disdain for what is termed journalism. Far from it; I have too intimate a knowledge of my epoch to repeat this absurd nonsense, this impertinent inanity against the Periodical Press. I know too well the work Providence has committed to it. Before this century shall run out journalism will be the whole press — the whole human thought. Since that prodigious multiplication which art has given to speech — multiplications to be multiplied a thousand-fold yet — mankind will write their books day by day, hour by hour, page by page. Thought will be spread abroad in the world with the rapidity of light; instantly conceived, instantly written, instantly understood at the extremities of the earth — it will spread from pole to pole. Sudden, instant, burning with the fervor of soul which made it burst forth, it will be the reign of the human soul in all its plenitude. It will not have time to ripen — to accumulate in a book; the book will arrive too late. The only book possible from today is a newspaper. [2]

Perhaps the largest conceivable revolution in information occurred on October 17, 1957, when Sputnik created a new environment for the planet. For the first time the natural world was completely enclosed in a man-made container. At the moment that the earth went inside this new artifact, Nature ended and Ecology was born. "Ecological" thinking became inevitable as soon as the planet moved up into the status of a work of art.

Ecological thinking and planning have always been native to preliterate man, since he lived not visually but acoustically. Instead of having external goals and objectives, he sought to maintain an equilibrium among the components of his environment

---

2 McLuhan, Marshall. "Joyce, Mallarmé and the Press." In *The Interior Landscape: The Literary Criticism of Marshall McLuhan*, edited by Eugene McNamara. New York: McGraw-Hill, 1969, p. 5.

in order to ensure survival. Paradoxically, electronic man shares much of the outlook of preliterate man, because he lives in a world of simultaneous information, which is to say, a world of resonance in which all data influence other data. Electronic and simultaneous man has recovered the primordial attitudes of the preliterate world and has discovered that to have a specialized goal or program merely invites conflict with all other specialized enterprises. "All the arts aspire to the condition of music," said Walter Pater, and under conditions of instant information the only possible rationale or means of order involves us in the musical structuring of experience.

Gutenberg man, in the sixteenth century, had achieved a new kind of detachment, thanks to the new intensity of visual experience deriving from the innovation of the printed word. This new visual stress impelled the men of that time to follow their individual goals, whether of learning or of travel and discovery, to the utmost extremes. A new race of visually oriented explorers of space and time emerged from the "caves" of the Gutenberg technology. The Gutenberg innovation enabled men to retrieve antiquity as never before. The new speed of the printing press created vast new political spaces and power structures based on the creation of new reading publics. The matrix of the press, with its assembly lines of moveable types, provided the archetypes of the industrial revolution and universal education.

The typical virtues of industrial and typographic man are radically revised and reformed when information moves at the speed of light. Whereas visual man had dreamed of distant goals and vast encyclopedic programs of learning, electronic man prefers dialogue and immediate involvement. Since nothing on earth can be distant at the speed of light, electronic man prefers the inner to the outer trip and the inner to the outer landscape. Simultaneous man is, paradoxically, traditional and simple in his tastes, preferring the human scale to the ancient grandeurs which are no longer difficult to achieve. Simultaneous man is acoustically rather than visually oriented, living in a world whose center is everywhere and whose margin is nowhere. Not for him the spirit of geometry or the spirit of quantity; instead of distant goals, he seeks pattern recognition, and instead of specialized jobs he prefers role-playing, with its flexibility and diversity. Indeed, at the moment of Sputnik the planet became a global theater in which there are no spectators but only actors. On Spaceship Earth there are no passengers; everybody is a member of the crew. These facts do not present themselves as ideals but as immediate realities.

To give both sides tends to ignore the possibility that there may be many more sides than two

It is noteworthy that the popular press as an art form has often attracted the enthusiastic attention of poets and aesthetes while rousing the gloomiest apprehensions in the academic mind. Let us look at the image of the newspaper as it still is today after a century of the telegraph. That image is organized not according to a story line but according to a date line. Like a symbolist poem, the ordinary newspaper page is an assembly of unconnected items in abstract mosaic form. Looked at in this way, it is plain that the newspaper had been a corporate poem for many years. It represents an inclusive image of community and a wide diversity of human interests. Minus the story line of the connected narrative, the newspaper has long had an oral and corporate quality which relates it to many of the traditional art forms of mankind. On every page of the newspaper, in the discontinuous mosaic of unrelated human items, there is a resonance that bespeaks universality, even in triviality. Robert Louis Stevenson said, "I could make an epic from a newspaper if I knew what to leave out."

The telegraph press was born in the age of symbolist poetry, the age of Edgar Allan Poe. Poe had confronted the poetic process in a way entirely consistent with the new electric speed of events and reporting. He simply pointed to the possibility of writing poetry backwards, starting with the effect desired and then proceeding to discover the "causes" or means for the desired effect.

Snyder and Morris [3] pointed to the same structural revolution in news writing that Poe and the Symbolists had discovered for poetry:

> Over the past hundred years the structure of the news story has undergone drastic modification. It is today a commonplace of American journalism that a news story must illustrate hind-to-end writing. Unlike other literary forms, the climax is at the beginning. The lead, or opening paragraph or paragraphs, gives the reader the essential facts. The body of the story is merely detailed expository material, its paragraph structure a series of separate units without transitions connecting them with what went before or what is to follow, and arranged in decreasing importance.

Symbolist art is the art of the rip-off. It is the experience of this active stripping that is the effect of symbolism. Merely as

---

3 Snyder, Louis L. and Richard B. Morris (Eds.). *A Treasury of Great Reporting.* New York: Simon & Schuster, 1962.

classified, separate items, things do not achieve symbolic status. It is so in the newspaper.

In the past decade there has come a recognizable change in the styles of reporting, now referred to as the "old journalism" and the "new journalism." The "old journalism" had sought objectivity; in presenting people and events it tried to achieve this by giving 'both sides' at once. To give the pro and the con, the good and the bad, has been for a century at least, the approved way of attaining judicial balance and fairness. To give both sides, however, tends to ignore the possibility that there may be many more sides than two, and as the means of access to information improved and as the means of processing information speeded up, the mere chiaroscuro of the light and the dark, the pro and the con, has tended to yield to nonvisual and subjective patterns of depth involvement by immersion in total situations. However, if the "old journalism" tended toward the salience of *figures* in men and events, the "new journalism" can be discerned as a preference for *ground* rather than *figure*. The "new journalism" offers not so much a view of men and events but a means of immersion in situations which involve many people simultaneously. Thus, Norman Mailer's account of the 1968 political conventions in Miami and Chicago is less concerned with the policies and the parties than with the experience of the hurly-burly of the conventions. [4] After all, the "you are there" immersion approach in journalism is only natural in the new surround of TV imagery: for TV brings the outside into the intimacy of the home, as it takes the private world of the home outside into the forum. The bounding line between the old and the new journalism seems to have been the popular line: "A funny thing happened to me on the way to the forum."

4 Mailer, Norman, *Miami and the Siege of Chicago*. New York: New American Library, 1968.

If the telegraph and the telephone revolutionized the patterns of information and speech in poetry and journalism, the advent of TV may carry us beyond speech altogether. One plausible projection by Gattegno [5] goes:

> Sight, even though used by all of us so naturally, has not yet produced its civilization. Sight is swift, comprehensive, simultaneously analytic and synthetic. It requires so little energy to function, as it does, at the speed of light, that it permits our minds to receive and hold an infinite number of items of information in a fraction of a second. With sight, infinities are given at once; wealth is its description. In contrast to the speed of light, we need time to talk and to express what we want to say. The inertia of photons is nil compared to the inertia of our muscles and chains of bones.
>
> Man has functioned as a seer and embraced vastnesses for millennia. But only recently, through television, has he been able to shift from the clumsiness of speech (however miraculous and far reaching) as means of expression and therefore of communication, to the powers of the dynamic, infinite visual expression, thus enabling him to share with everybody immense dynamic wholes in no time.
>
> Even if for some time speech will remain the most common way of letting others know what we know, we can foresee the coming of an era where the processing of visual material will be as easy as our comprehension of talk but swifter because of the former's lack of inertia; and through its spatialization by electrons, we shall be able to share vast conscious experiences at once. Today large novels are needed for this.

---

5 Gattegno, Caleb. *Towards a Visual Culture*. New York: Outerbridge and Dienstfrey, 1969, p. 4.

Xerox comes as a reverse flip as the end of the Gutenberg cycle; whereas Gutenberg made everybody a reader, Xerox makes everybody a publisher

Without trying to look ahead one hundred years — without looking even one year ahead, if we merely *Take Today* [6] for a look at the changing nature of human organization as reflected in things and in newspapers — it is possible to see some striking new patterns. The release of the Pentagon papers and the Ellsberg investigation point to one of these patterns, one directly related to the matter of Xerox. Xerox, as a new service in connection with written and printed materials, is so decentralized, accessible, and inexpensive that it results in making the ordinary person a publisher, if he so chooses.

Quite apart from its threat to the publishing business and to copyright regulations, Xerox has two other features. On the one hand, it has created the large committee as a new means of decision-making, because it permits uniform briefing and position papers for all. On the other hand, it has created, also on a large scale, the underground press. [In passing it might be helpful to mention apropos the underground press that its relation to the public, or above-ground press, is somewhat similar to the old and new journalism. Speaking in gestalt psychology terms, the press can be seen in relation to *figure* and *ground*, and in psychology as well as in journalism, the *ground* is usually subliminal, relative to the *figure*. Under conditions of electric simultaneity the *ground* of any *figure* tends to become more and more noticeable. Perhaps it all began with cubism and the discovery that by eliminating the

---

6 McLuhan, Marshall, and Barrington Nevitt. *Take Today: The Executive as Dropout*. New York: Harcourt, Brace, Jovanovitch Inc., 1972.

merely visual or rational relations between services, by presenting the inside and the underside at the same time as the outside, the public became totally involved and aware in a multisensuous way. As new media continue to proliferate, the nature of "news" will naturally change too, along with the perpetually renewed revolution in information speeds and patterns.]

Position papers are secret or confidential documents for the attention of committees, and any office boy can publish these, no matter how top secret they may be. The Pentagon Papers were position papers which may or may not have been studied or discussed by a Congressional committee. They are "the news behind the news," which used to be considered muckraking but has now become an ordinary dimension of journalism, such as nourishes the underground press and which, in turn, affects the forms and publics of the regular press. What has happened since the old muckraking days of the 1920s is that espionage, whether political or commercial, has become the largest business in the world, and we take it for granted that the modern newspaper depends on "bugging" the whole community. In fact, we expect the press to "bug" the world and to challenge and penetrate all privacy and identity, whether private or corporate.

Among the unexpected features of the information revolution are the extraordinary diminution of private identity and egotistic conviction, as a result of major involvement in the lives of other people, and the extraordinary enlargement of the public sector. We have moved into an age in which everybody's activities affect everybody else, and therefore the whole matter of privacy is suspect, even as it is impractical. One result has been a relaxing of private morals (sometimes referred to as "permissiveness") and at the same time an extraordinary new intensity in public morals. This change is well reflected in the Watergate affair. In Washington, as elsewhere, laxity of private standards is expected, but the same private standards no longer extend to the image of the President. Under electric conditions it is not possible to extend the laxity of private life into the public domain; rather, a new absolutism in the public domain is felt to be mandatory.

The U.S. happens to be the country in which the private and specialized had been allowed the utmost development. Quite dramatically, therefore, the "bugging" of private lives, long taken for granted in the commercial, the political, and the military establishments, has suddenly become the means of revealing the bankruptcy of public morals.

A spectacular paradigm of the information revolution has been developed for the world at large by the Watergate affair. While it seems to specialize in matters of political espionage and image-building, it also draws attention to the fact that the entire educational and commercial establishments, as much as the political and military establishments, depend on data banks of total information concerning both producers and consumers, both the governors and the governed. The Watergate affair makes it quite plain that the entire planet has become a whispering gallery, with a large portion of mankind engaged in making its living by keeping the rest of mankind under surveillance. The FBI includes among its responsibilities keeping under surveillance individual members of the CIA. We thus have a complete scheme of baby-sitters for the baby-sitters — chaperones for chaperones

— and it is the business of every commercial establishment to keep all other commercial establishments under surveillance as a minimal condition of survival.

Xerox is a new kind of decentralized service which dissolves privacy and creates many new forms of human association, whether in the classroom or in the legislature or in the press. Whereas Gutenberg had created a service that extended to whole nations, he had at the same time invented a form of hardware that fostered new forms of central organization, including a price system and the markets that came with it. What Arnold Toynbee had discerned as "etherialization" — the tendency in our time to do more and more with less and less — is part of the electronic information revolution of "software," which has the opposite effect of decentralizing. While hardware requires uniformity of product to pay for a centralized operation, the electronic form of information service permits not only decentralizing of organizations but a wide diversity of products without additional expenditure.

If book and hardware sales need to be large to defray expenses, electronic publishing by Xerox can dispense with large-scale publics and markets almost entirely. Even more easily than by hand-press, a writer can publish a few copies of his work for his friends by simply multiplying the typescript. In fact, Xerox completes the work of the typewriter. A poet composing at the typewriter is "publishing" his work, as it were. Xerox gives to this fact a new meaning.

Electric speed may already have violated human scale, tending as it does to transport man instantly everywhere

In the early days of the book, Montaigne thought of printing as a kind of flip from the confessional to the expressional:

> Letter-writing . . . is a kind of work in which my friends think I have some ability. And I would have preferred to adopt this form to publish my sallies, if I had had someone to talk to. I needed what I once had, a certain relationship to lead me on, sustain me, and raise me up. . . . I would have been more attentive and confident, with a strong friend to address, than I am now, when I consider the various tastes of a whole public. And if I am not mistaken, I would have been more successful. . . . Amusing notion: many things that I would not want to tell anyone, I tell the public; and for my most secret knowledge and thoughts I send my most faithful friends to a bookseller's shop. [7]

Montaigne here draws attention to the book as a kind of message in a bottle: secretly dispatched, to an unknown public of potential acquaintances. His thoughts on this subject help to reveal an aspect of the newspaper as well, because there is a special meaning of publication as a form of "put on"; the writer, whether of a diary or a newspaper column, is engaged in a very special way in putting on his public as a mask.

Ersilia: *Why wasn't it true? I wanted to kill myself!*
Ludovico: *Yes! But in doing so you created an entire novel —*
Ersilia: *(fearfully) What do you mean, created? Do you think I made it all up?*
Ludovico: *No, no, I meant, in me. You created it in me, without knowing it, by telling your story.*

---

7 Frame, Donald M. *Montaigne: A Biography*. New York: Harcourt, Brace &World, 1965, p. 83.

Ersilia:	*When they found me in that park —*
Ludovico:	*Yes, and then later, in the hospital. Forgive me, but how can you imply you were nobody? For one thing, you existed in the pity everyone felt for you when they read your story in the paper. You can't imagine the impression it made when it was published, the interest you aroused all over the city.*
Ersilia:	*(anxiously) Do you still have it?*
Ludovico:	*Yes, I think so. I must have saved it.*
Ersilia:	*Find it, find it! Let me see it!*
Ludovico:	*No, why should you get all upset again?*
Ersilia:	*Let me see it! Please! I want to read it, I want to read what they wrote about me.* [8]

The most secret diary, even that of Samuel Pepys, written in a code which remained unbroken for centuries — even such a diary is for the writer a mask or a vortex of energy which increases his power over the language; for our mother tongue is itself a corporate mask of energy which is stepped up by the act of writing and, once again, by the act of publication. In the early days of printing, Montaigne saw this action as both putting on the public and the taking off of his privacy:

> I owe a complete portrait of myself to the public. The wisdom of my lesson is wholly in truth, in freedom, in reality . . . of which propriety and ceremony are daughters, but bastard daughters.
>
> . . . Whoever would wean man of the folly of such a scrupulous verbal superstition would do the world no great harm. Our life is part folly, part wisdom. Whoever writes about it only reverently and according to the rules leaves out more than half of it.

8 Pirandello, Luigi. "To Clothe the Naked." In *To Clothe the Naked and Two Other Plays*, translated by William Murray. New York: E. P. Dutton, 1962.

Montaigne had discovered the paradox that the larger the public, the greater the premium on the self-confessional.

There is something rather mysterious about the process of the put-on" which is inseparable from communication. Baudelaire's famous phrase, "*hypocrite lecteur, mon semblable, mon frère,*" [9] captures the entire process. The reader is hypocrite in the very act of putting on the author's poem as his mask, for in reading the poem he is perceiving the world in a very special way, using what another poet, S. T. Coleridge, called "willing suspension of disbelief for the moment." When we put on any man-made mask such as painting, poem, or music, or when we read a book or a newspaper, we are looking at the world in a very special way, altering our own perceptions by an artistic act of faith in the process in which we are engaged.

The second part of Baudelaire's phrase, "*mon semblable, mon frère,*" draws attention to the reciprocal part of the action. Whereas the reader or the user of any form puts it on as his mask, as an extension of his own perception and energy, the author or maker has also to put on his public, the potential reader or user of whatever he has made. The maker tends to project his own image as the mask of the user or reader which he endeavors to "put on." This complex process of communication, by which the medium is "put on" by its users in order that they may experience some alteration and extension of their own perception and powers, includes the "putting on" of the user by the medium. Commercially, this latter operation is referred to as "giving the public what it wants" or "the customer is always right." The complexity of this process is such that even literary critics have despaired of ever unravel-

9 Envoy to the reader of *Les fleurs du mal*.

ling it. Critics of the press, on the other hand, are accustomed to labeling the whole thing as degrading, even as Shakespeare did with his own profession of acting.

One thing that needs to be noted in both connections is the great increase of the sense of power on the part of both the maker and the user. Since the process in question is at the very heart of the communication activity, it is certain to remain central to the issue so long as readers are human and not merely robots. Since "human scale" is indispensable for human satisfactions, the future of the press must inevitably retain this dimension. At present, electric speed may already have violated human scale, tending as it does to transport man instantly everywhere. When you are "on the air" you are simultaneously here and in many other places in a manner that is discarnate and angelic, to say the least.

At instant speeds . . . the public begins to participate directly in actions which it had previously heard about at a distance in place or time

It is time to ask ourselves: "What is news?" When a visitor stepped into an antique store, he asked "What's new?" His jocular query draws attention to the fact that we live in the age of the fake antique, which is itself a form of the replay. Is not "news" itself a replay in the newspaper medium of events that have occurred in some other medium, and does not this replay quality in reporting urge us to narrow the margin between the event and the replay? Does not this make us define news as "the latest"?

However, in the new age of the instant replay, news takes on a totally new dimension that is almost metaphysical. A ball game or a horse race can now be replayed for its meaning, as it were, minus the experience. During the actual experience the issue may have been in doubt, but, as the poet explains, "we can have the experience and miss the meaning." In fact, such is the nature of experience that it is almost inevitable that we do miss the meaning. The "meaning" or the relation to ourselves of a particular event, may not come home to us until much later. However, with the instant replay of our own or others' experiences, it is now possible to have the meaning without the experience. Referees and judges may wait for the replay in order to render a decision. They have had the experience and are merely waiting for the meaning or the relation of the experience to themselves and to others.

The quality of the instantaneous in the replay of experience is somewhat like the difference between cognition and recognition. Recognition may come somewhat after the event and is a form of awareness in which we say: "Oh, I didn't realize it was you" or "Oh, now I see what it's all about." Recognition is an altogether higher order of awareness from cognition, and yet it is now taken for granted as a normal feature of daily life in the electric age. Newspapers have long used this instant dimension in experience, at least since the time of the telegraph and the telephone, which have been with us for many decades. The mysterious thing about this kind of speed-up of information, whereby the gap is closed between the experience and the meaning, is that the public begins to participate directly in actions which it had previously heard about at a distance in place or time. At instant speeds the audience becomes actor, and the spectators become participants.

On Spaceship Earth or in the global theater the audience and the crew become actors, producers rather than consumers. They seek to program events rather than to watch them. As in so many other instances, these "effects" appear before their "causes." At instant speeds the cause and effect are at least simultaneous, and it is this dimension which naturally suggests, to all those who are accustomed to it, the need to anticipate events hopefully rather than to participate in them fatalistically. The possibility of public participation becomes a sort of technological imperative which has been called "Lapp's Law": "If it can be done, it's got to be done" — a kind of siren wail of the evolutionary appetite.

At the Moment of Sputnik the Planet became a Global Theater in which there are no Spectators but only Actors
Marshall McLuhan - Unbound (05)

ISBN: 1-58423-051-7
Library of Congress Control Number 2005927213

Marshall McLuhan Unbound Project Editors
Eric McLuhan, W. Terrence Gordon

Published in United States in October 2005 by
Gingko Press, Inc.
5768 Paradise Drive, Suite J · Corte Madera, CA 94925
(415) 924-9615 · Fax (415) 924-9608
email: books@gingkopress.com
http://www.gingkopress.com

Design, packaging and production: Die Gestalten Verlag, Berlin
Layout and Typography: onlab, Berlin
Fonts: *Dolly* by Underware, *Bullet* by House Industries
Production: Martin Bretschneider, Vinzenz Geppert
Art direction: Robert Klanten

Made in Germany